D1692549

Meditation for Two

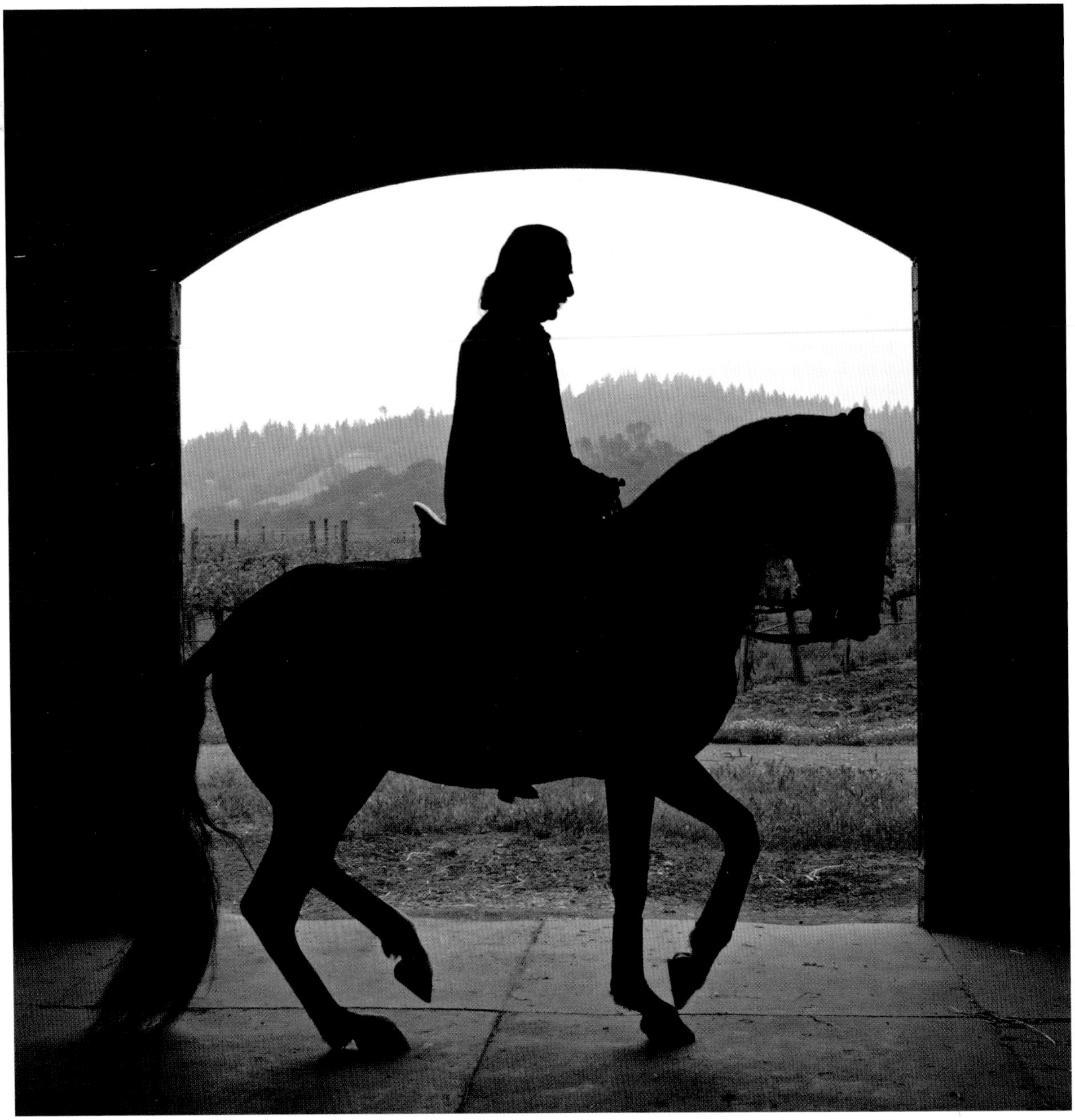

Meditation for Two

Searching for and Finding Communion with the Horse

Dominique Barbier and Keron Psillas

Trafalgar Square
North Pomfret, Vermont

First published in 2011 by

Trafalgar Square Books

North Pomfret, Vermont 05053

Printed in China

Copyright 2011 by Dominique Barbier and Keron Psillas

All rights reserved. No part of this book maybe reproduced, by any means, without written permission of the publisher, except by a reviewer quoting for a review in a magazine, newspaper, or web site.

ISBN: 978-1-57076-497-4

Library of Congress Control Number: 2011934729

Book design by Keron Psillas

Cover design by RM Didier

10 9 8 7 6 5 4 3 2

It is rare to see a rider who is truly passionate about the horse and his training, taking a profound interest in dressage with self-abnegation, and making this extraordinarily subtle work one of the dominant motivations of his life.

Mestre Nuno Oliveira

from Dominique

for Debra, Domina, and Tianna,
   and for my Dad and my Mom
and Keron, my soul sister

from Keron

for Dominique, whose beautiful heart and
   ageless soul inspires and heals, as ever

for Sam, with gratitude for your elegant aesthetic
   and lasting friendship

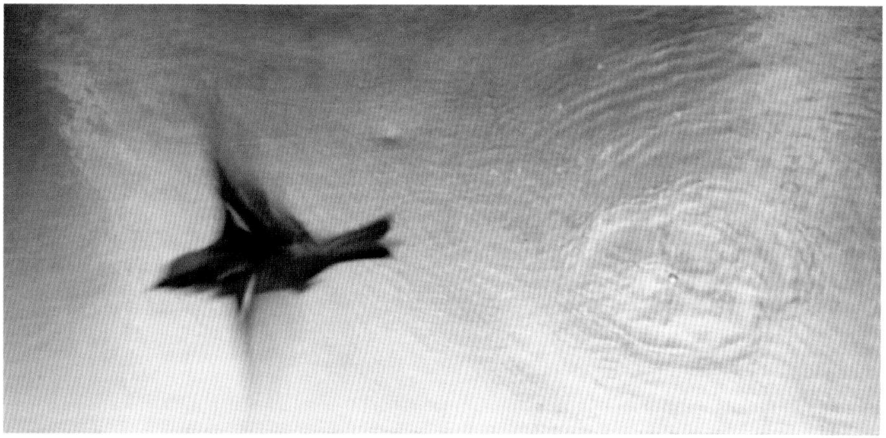

The master, thus draws the apprentice slowly away from preconceived ideas, theories, and even history, toward life as fullness of present action.

Ken Beittel

We ride as we are. We bring ourselves to the dance. Consider the self you would offer your partner, your beloved. In the endeavor to create awareness of self, we step onto the path that leads to Grace.

What better purpose for a life than to hold the space for beauty? Dominique does more though. He invites us in. With a deceptively simple mantra: direction, rhythm, bend, lightness. If we accept we will discover awareness, calm, and acceptance, and for many, joy.

Nearly twenty years ago, Dominique took my hand and asked me to join him on this path. The cosmic twins, the brother and sister, had found each other.

There have been detours and snares, grief and loss. But the abiding constant has been love; the love from my horses ~ my partners, and the love of family and friends. Through all, my awareness that love is has sustained me.

From this knowing springs hope and limitless gratitude. And from gratitude I have had Grace revealed. I have learned to embody yes and honor the power of my being to create a meaningful life.

Thank you, Dominique, for your love of the horse and your unending desire to heal the horses and to offer this teaching to your students.

My most cherished photographs are a communication of spirit. I offer this conversation in thanks for the exchange and connection we continue to share.

Avante! Com Coragem! Tudo é beleza.
KP

L'amour, c'est ne pas une histoire de tête, c'est une histoire de cœur.

Love is not the story of the head, it is the story of the heart.

Today I woke up early with a great urge to write. My dog, Lillie, is snug around my neck. The sun is going to shine today. My pen works on its own. Later, when I look up, the grape vines all around me are being pruned. The old is cut in order for the new to grow and bear new fruit in the warmth and vibrancy of the earth in order. What a wonderful day. Thank you, God, for this morning.

Please remind me that there is nothing that you and I cannot do together.

DB

Nous pouvons, d'abord, trouver notre sourire et apprendre à l'utiliser.

We can, early on, find our smile and learn to use it.

Too many times we allow our first thoughts in the morning to be negative ones. How much better, then, to discipline ourselves to allow our first thoughts to be happy ones. After all, we can always deal with the less pleasant ones later. Perhaps we can maintain this sense of well-being throughout the day. We can, early on, find our smile, and learn to use it through discipline, meditation, visualization, and love.

This book is a reflection about the love of horses and how much they care and want us to be better. It is my belief that were we to allow ourselves to listen, were we to allow them to speak, they would surely have offered such a book to us.

Because the nature of the horse demands it, this is a mystical, metaphysical book. For horses, our healers, are also in need of healing. And yet, someone must lead the dance. We can help by attending to their creature comforts ~ putting them in a safe place, physically, by removing obvious dangers. But more importantly, mentally, we can help the horses heal by shifting our preconceptions and expectations.

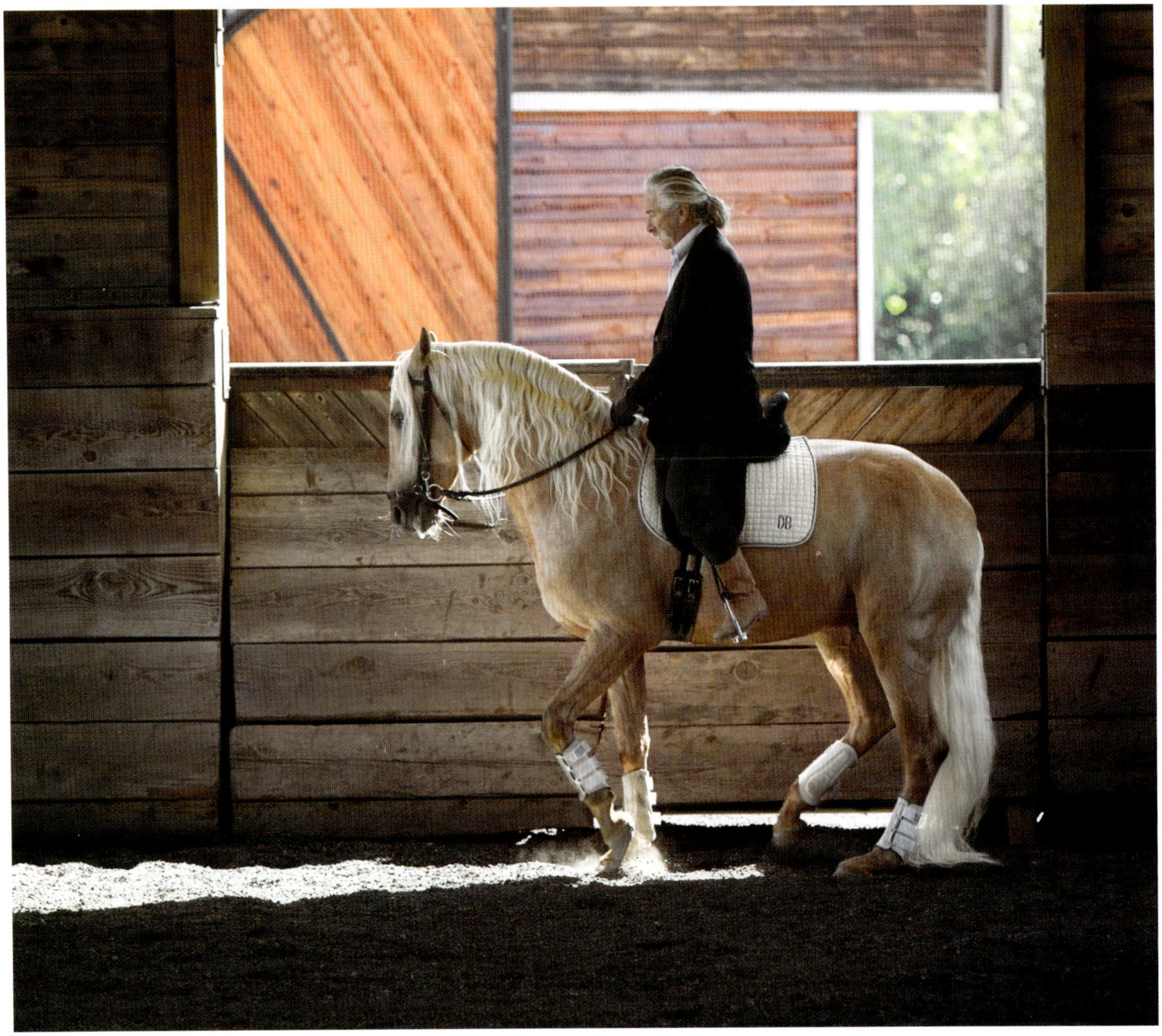
DB

For the past thirty years, I have been very fortunate. I have worked with thousands of horses, sometimes as many as twenty a day. Because of the timeframe imposed on my clinic situations, where I work an individual horse twice a day, for two to nine days every three months (ideally with another professional helping in between), I have been obliged to rethink many of my original approaches. This has helped me focus and expand my teaching, my career, and my life, in a profound way.

Horses and humans: the idea of separation first and then a coming together when mutual respect and understanding are attained is too simplistic, though not to be ignored. Rather, if I can say, it is the sense of oneness first, and then how to remain in that oneness that I believe is the essence of successful and symbiotic interaction between human and horse.

To put it more informally, perhaps, I think the question now is still do you want to dance?, but additionally, what dance shall we do today? The notion of the centaur takes on an added dimension: it is not just human and horse metaphorically and aesthetically, but mentally and spiritually bound in a deeply resonant way.

Les chevaux sont le miroir de notre ame.

Horses are the mirror of our soul.

Let go of old notions of man's superiority, of man taming the beast; recognize and respect who they are; revere them. But first, look inside yourself. Horses bring a purer spirit to the equation in some ways than do we, because while man has, for centuries, been searching for God, horses are already on the sacred path to enlightenment; here and now, within and without. People think that horses have problems with concentration, when in reality, ours is the more undisciplined mind.

Horses live in the here and now. Most students are unable to understand that concept. Horses do not predict and are selective in their memories; they do not dwell on the past or the future, though our own inadequacies can provoke action and reaction with both positive and negative results.

The horse must trust the student. He must accept and enjoy a comfortable position, something that does not always come naturally. In turn, the student must trust the horse, both physically and mentally. If your riding mentality is based in fear, the horse cannot believe, understand, or feel comfortable with you. Panic and evasions follow. A void in the student creates a void in the horse. Horses are the mirror of your soul, of who

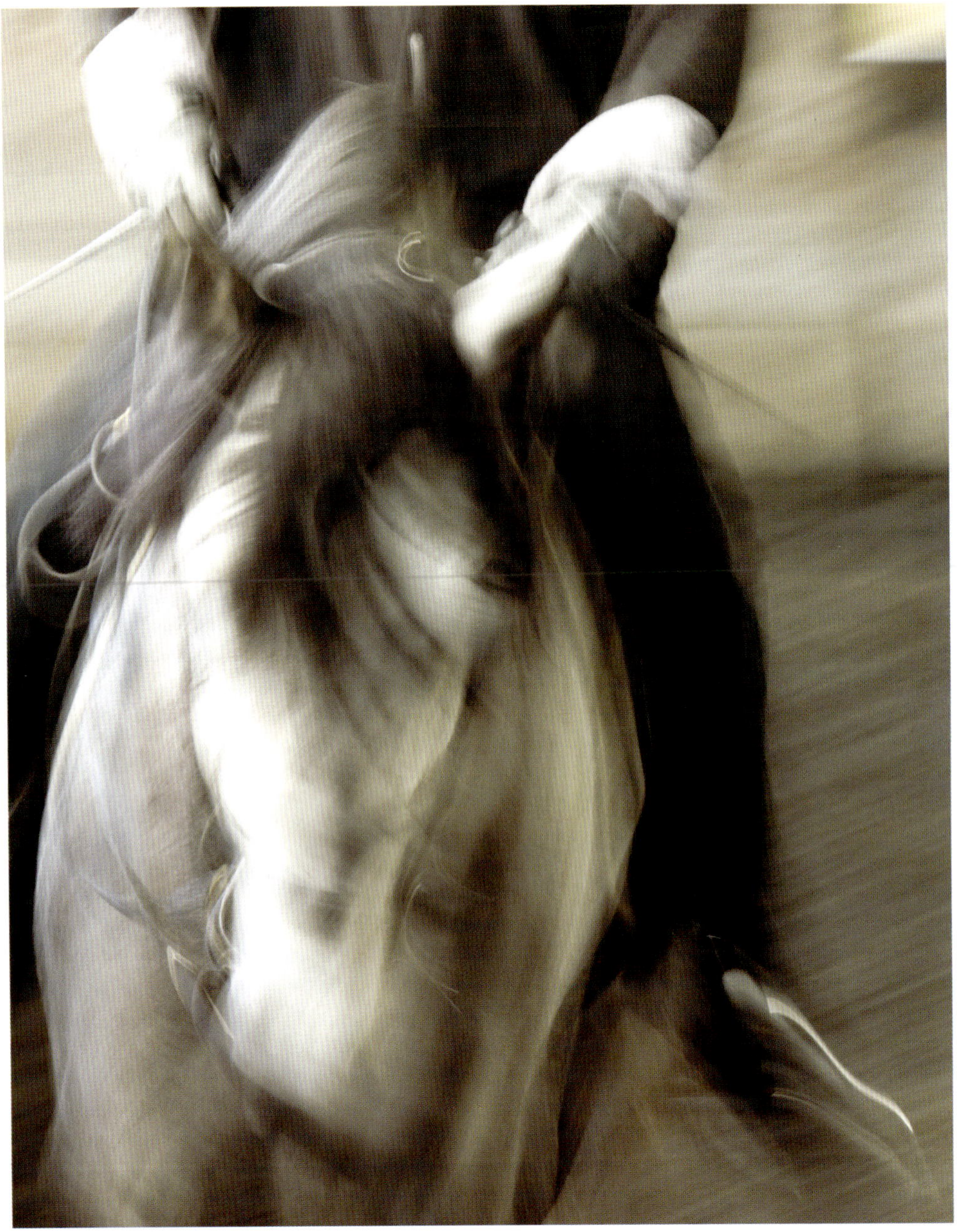

you really are. It is your reflection that you see through their eyes. Through them, you can more easily come to know yourself. Through you, they can more easily come to fulfill themselves.

The attitude that we are the only or best conduit of energy is a limiting one. The horse is already here. We must learn to be here. Our undisciplined minds and our egos cause us to live in the past or in the future and we must remind ourselves constantly of the goal of self-realization. Unlike the horse, we are so busy doing, we forget simply to be, we are so busy working, we forget to enjoy. Horses demand our presence, and this mental discipline in turn allows communication and oneness to happen. They teach us to be in and stay in the present, to share the same vibrations, the same space, the same energy. They teach us to replace organized unhappiness, unfulfilled dreams and expectations with the attachment and appreciation of the very moment. When acceptance and grace flow between horse and rider, the centaur can exist.

Élargir notre foi et ouvrir notre cœur.

We complete the circle when we widen our faith and open our hearts.

Fear is a great inhibitor to successful interaction with the horse ~ or with humans. It takes many forms. Perhaps the most elemental fear is man's primary concern with being ungrounded.

It is curious that this should be so, since it is obvious that we, all of us ~ all living forms ~ share an energy and a synergy that stems from the complete and irrefutable continual interchange of life forces and simply physical exchanges. Horses and humans consist of much more than their horseness or their humaness. Every living thing exists within every other, and all contain and retain all the forces of the earth and of the heavens.

So it is important to accept that the physical ungrounding of man when he sits astride a horse is of no real consequence and should not be fear provoking, as the introduction of the equine conduit can only augment the natural synergy flowing from earth to man. When we learn to be secure in the amplified strength that flows through both beings, when we learn to embrace the power that stems from a partnership so easily formed but so rarely acknowledged, we will have achieved a level of psychic well-being that can only be beneficial to all. It is ironic, then, that we speak so casually of our fears as being groundless, when in fact, our fears are so often the result of finally feeling true grounding.

It is too often the nature of man to fear the loss of what he perceives as control, both mental and physical. We are so often trained to trust our heads, not our hearts, to trust intellect over instinct. With the horse, there is no such conflict. They exist in the here and now. Their egos, if they can be said to have any, reflect more the recognition of a sort of pecking order in the universe, a knowledge of where they stand in relation to every other part of the world, animate and inanimate. Where our own egos regularly allow fear and negativity to interfere with our ability to let go and form spiritual connections, horses possess an incalculable ability to function as conduits of connection. Where we analzye, where we try to explain, where we try to re-create, where we try to simply be, horses are already there ~ waiting for us to walk through the open door, to follow the path of spiritual oneness, to allow healing energy to come in.

For A Friend

Such a tentative, gentle spirit
with liquid amber, softly searching eyes,
let your passions come out to play,
　let your longing loose for a while.
You are safe, you are loved.
Tell me your secrets
　I'll hold them in my heart,
I am safe, I am love,
Let me touch, as you have touched.

La porte est toujours là, toujours ouverte. Il n'est jamais trop tard pour entrer.

The door is always there, always open. It is never too late to step through.

Every time in my learning I felt a breakthrough, I have opened a door to find my horse on the other side, waiting, saying, "It's about time; I have been waiting for you." After time, there would be another breakthrough, and there he was again. The only limits I have found have been my own.

Of course, your ego is telling you that such breakthroughs are your own doing. That is your ego's job. As far as he is concerned, he is acting in your best interest. That is why you must be compassionate with him, because the truth is that to become one with your horse, you ultimately leave your ego behind, which is a pretty scary idea. But to allow the centaur to emerge, we have to create both space and the attitude where we can accept the lessons that our horses are trying to teach us. By letting go of the ego's conception of self, we can form another self, this one more physically able, mentally aware and spiritually open; we can create instead of recreate, we can take the empty space and fill it more profoundly, more graciously, and with the simple certitude that

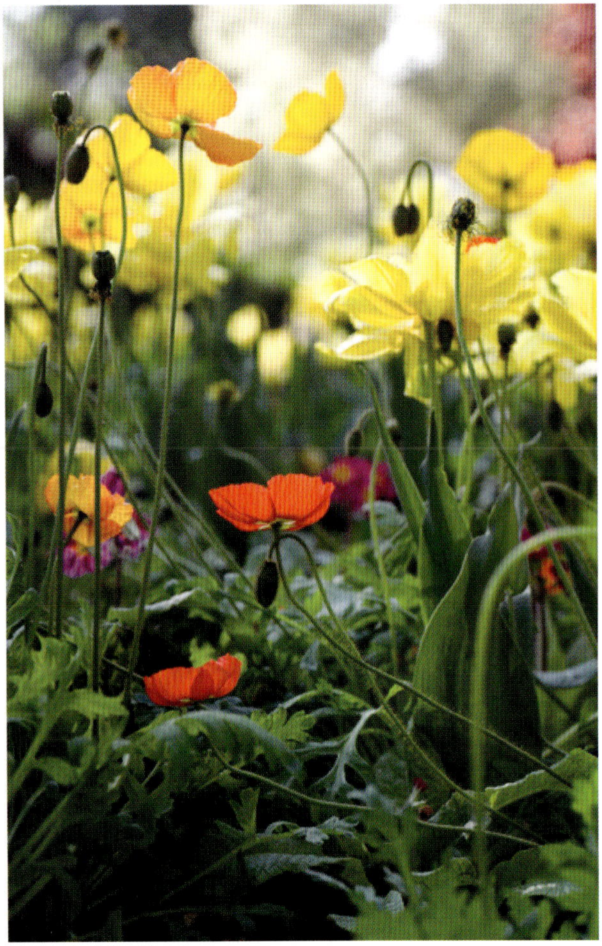

we are now, finally, approaching true connection with the horse, anad therefore, the universe. We learn to trust. We learn to be. We celebrate.

How lucky we are to know the passage, how lucky we are to know the horses are with us to lead the way. How lucky we are to just be with them. In a world of violence and chaos, in this time of Kali Yuga, where confusion reigns, let us be thankful we have those thoughtful, gentle beings sharing life with us.

Let us try to understand them and protect them, as we will understand ourselves better and feel oneness and joy.

> *All things share the same breath, the beast, the tree, the man. The air shares its spirit with all the life it supports. If all the beasts were gone, man would die from loneliness of spirit, for whatsoever happens to the beast happens to the man. All things are connected. Whatever befalls the earth befalls the sons of the earth.*
>
> Chief Seattle

Sans la equilibre symetrique de l'univers nous ne sommes rien. Avec lui, nous sommes tout et de façon heureuse, nous somme un avec le cheval et les anges.

Without the symmetric balance of the universe we are nothing. With it, we are everything, and, blessedly, one with the horse and the angels.

Horses and man share more than physical space. We interact in a way that is special among animals. We are symbiotic healers. It has been my experience that if we help the horse achieve a higher degree of physical and mental comfort, the healing powers become much stronger. Through the gentle techniques of work in hand we can find mental and physical positions that they enjoy. Healing energy can replace the concept of fitness or progressive training. Helping the horse to a different level of consciousness, one that allows him to produce a different position, that leads to a different movement produces the strength that can come only with relaxation and a sense of well being. The new consciousness that comes to them and the new healing energy that is then unleashed allow rider and horse to meet as one. We have invited the horse to show us the access to oneness and when we arrive at the level of detachment needed to accept that access, we find peace within, harmony and

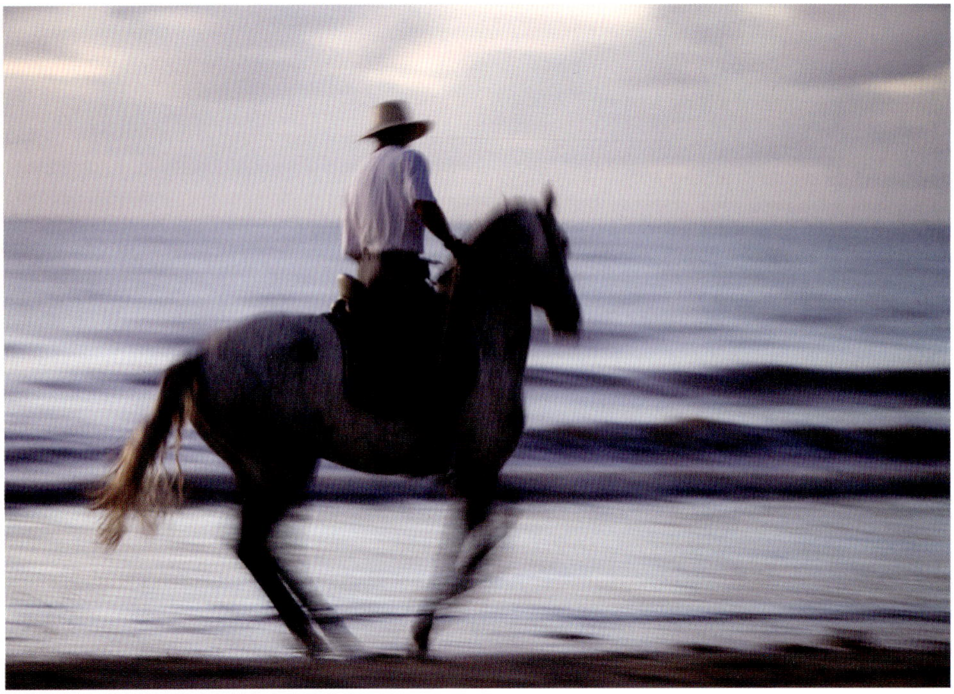

oneness with the outside. Only then can we start to see ourselves for what we are and them for what they are, parts of the centaur; a superior consciousness where no separation exists, an empowering feeling of Divine Presence.

A Cup of Tea

Nan-in, a Japanese master during the Meiji era, received a university professor who came to inquire about Zen.

Nan-in served tea. He poured his visitor's cup full, and then kept on pouring.

The professor watched the overflow until he no longer could restrain himself. "It is overfull. No more will go in!"

"Like this cup," Nan-in said, "you are full of your own opinions and speculations. How can I show you Zen unless you first empty your cup?"

Il n'y a aucune différence entre celui qui regarde et celui qui est regardé.

There is no difference between the one who is looking and the one who is looked at.

I consider the shoulder-in the miracle movement. But I prefer to call it shoulders-in. The outside shoulder must be included in the movement, in our feeling of the movement. From the daily work for the original work-in-hand around one pillar, a technique centuries old, we need to understand why this is such a revealing movement, why it is such a powerful tool. The simplest answer is that it gives the horse a feeling of togetherness, then of independence. He learns where his legs and his body are in relation to himself and to the rider. This knowledge offers security to him and, in turn, imparts an additional, undeniable mental strength, as any successful human athlete can attest. Taking away doubt and fear allows increased mental maturity, and with it, the ability to confidently take on a bigger project, to tackle a more complex problem. This different consciousness, this additional self-confidence creates mental and physical generosity. The horse is a natural healer, a natural giver; when a being ~ horse or human ~ is validated and touched by love, his healing abilities and his desire to share his gifts are expanded. We need to expand our own

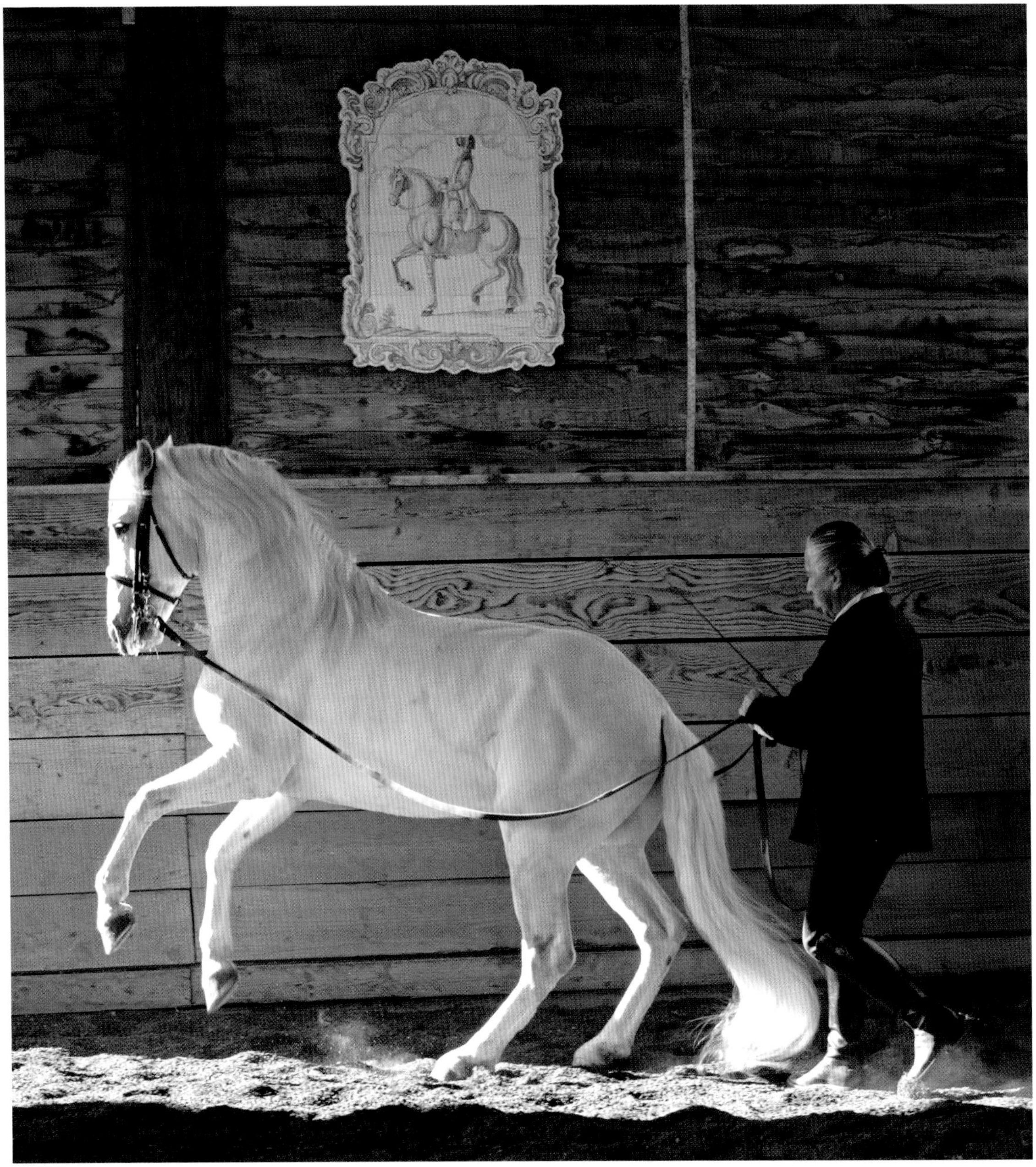

abilities, to be compassionate and open, disciplined and focused. An undisciplined mind is like a young green horse ~ full of life, scattered and uncensored. All manner of achievement is possible when the horse, like your mind, comes to the calm knowledge of self and respect of others. Together these notions bring harmony and joy. Gratitude and reverence allow us to be and feel that there is nothing we cannot do. Remember, then, to say thank you. The open mind and the readiness for the path to further enlightenment will create real-life miracles.

Un jour, dans la joie, un jour uni.

One day, in joy, one day as one.

To examine the movement from a purely physical standpoint, first there is the crossing of the leg, which can be compared to a child's crawling; both open neurological passages to the brain, both provide valuable information about who and what the horse, the child, is, particularly in relationship to itself and to its surroundings. When the horse crosses his legs, two other things happen: at a maximum of crossing, the shoulder blade opens and at the maximum of spreading, the shoulder blade closes. Why is this important? The horse does not possess collar bones, there is no boney articulation between the shoulder blade and the thoracic cage, which means that the shoulder blade is attached to the body by muscle, tendon, and ligament. When he is tense or stressed, and these muscles, tendons, and ligaments are rigid, they are working against the movement. The horse is blocked. Only in relaxation can they work efficiently. Therefore, stride after stride, crossing after crossing, the horse relaxes, allowing the maximum of elasticity, of flexibility. You must be sure that the horse is willing to be flexible in order to help him achieve a comfortable position. The hind legs crossing in the movement

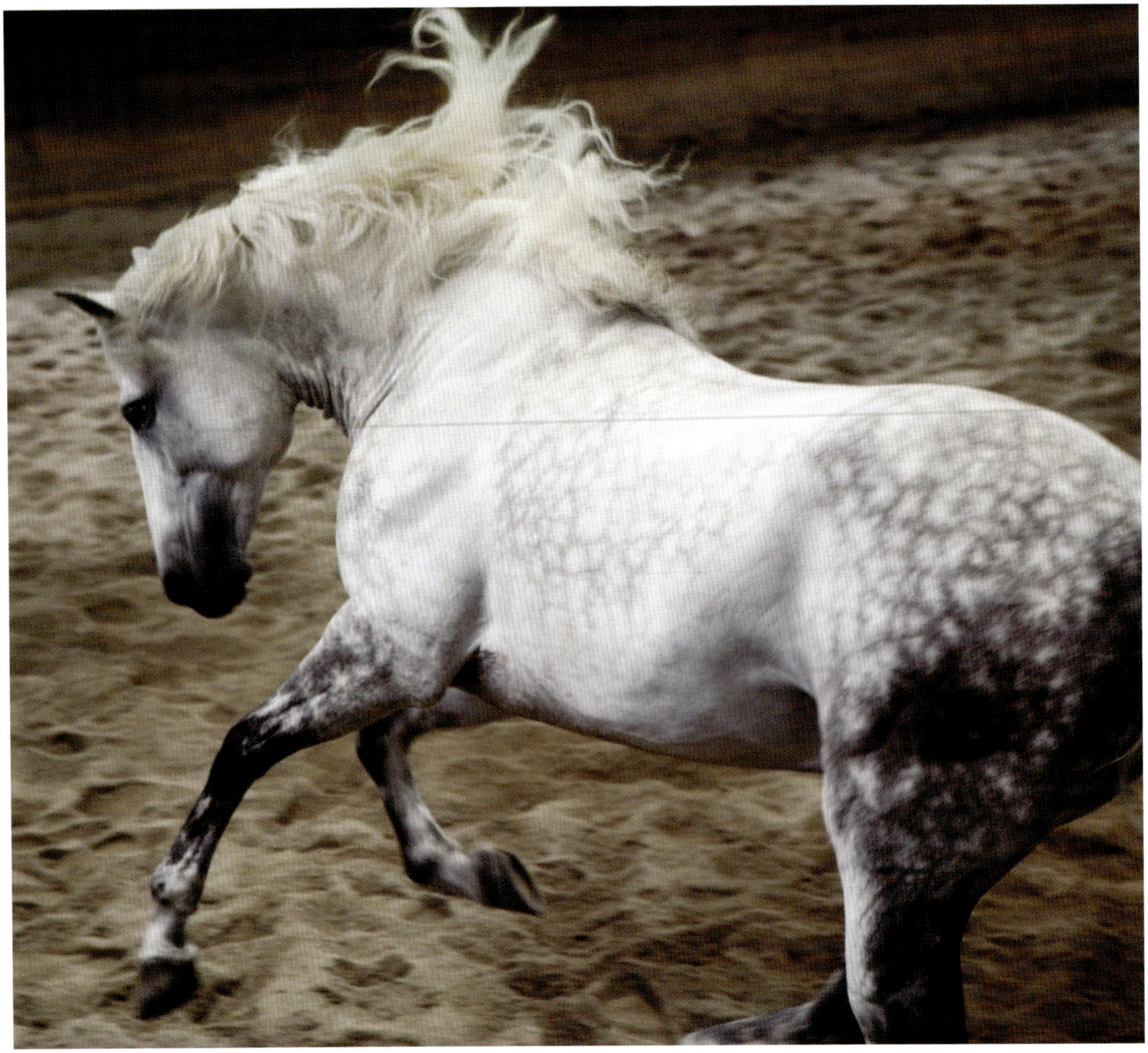

indicates a willingness and ability to carry some of the body weight usually incorrectly carried by the front end. This is the beginning of engagement. It is the beginning of the coming through. While you ride, therefore, you should experience the same feeling - loosen your back - to enhance the movement from your horse. He will tell you when and where he is comfortable. The horse is a performer, we just suggest. We have an idea of the blueprint; let him build from it.

Catch the vigorous horse of your mind.

- Zen saying

Nous tenons leurs vies dans nos mains. Puisse nos mains être toujours guidées par la douceur.

We hold their lives in our hands.
Would that our hands are always guided truly, gently.

I believe that the horses want us to know ourselves better. They teach us love and compassion. They understand our limitations. They make us feel conflict, they make us realize our fears, and they help us to figure out and neutralize negativity. They teach us to let go. But this working without a safety net is a scary concept. If we fall, do we expect them to catch us? I believe they do just that. The emotional free fall we expect is arrested by harmony and enlightenment. Remember how horses react to different personalities. They can take care of you or challenge you. They will adapt the challenge to your ability. The more you think you know, the bigger the challenge. The same horse nurses the beginner, that makes sure that he/she is safe will challenge an overindulged ego that needs a reminder about his diet. They teach us structure, self-awareness, and grace. When man communicates with the horse it is on so many levels, but the most important is the

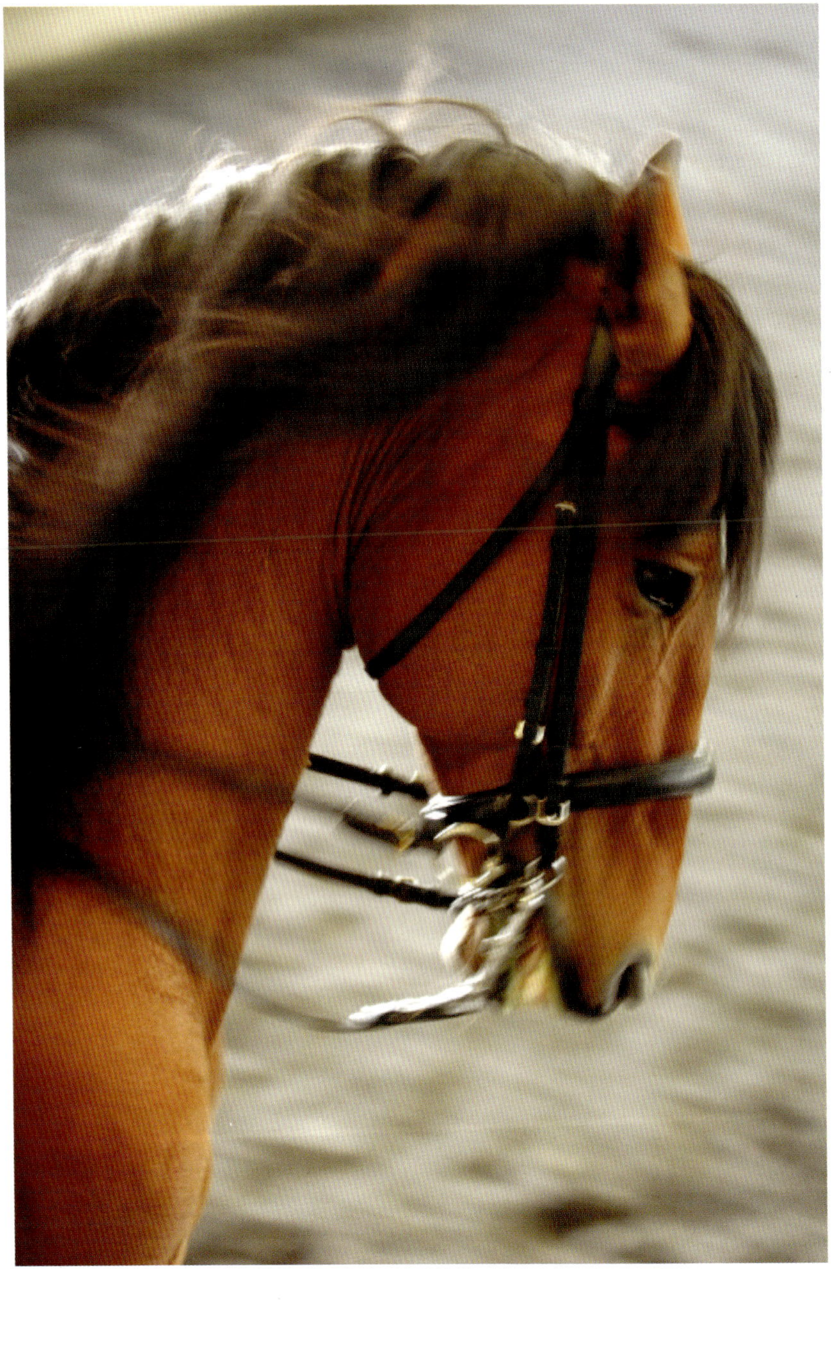

spiritual. Because above all, the horses are spiritual creatures. Who is closer to God than the horse? Who flies so without wings, who speaks so eloquently without words, who imparts such true knowledge without avarice?

Teach Me

What voice will be heard?
How must I speak these words?

Teach me the way to speak
  the truth in my heart...

To fill, to lift, to inspire.
Teach me to speak so that
others will trust,
  reach higher.

*Leçons de calme, en silence menant
à la clarté ; leçons de clarté, menant
à la lumière.*

Lessons of stillness, leading to clarity; lessons of clarity leading to light.

A true teacher does not improve mediocrity, he facilitates a true change of consciousness. Where we see so many students become disillusioned and so many horses frustrated is prior to that change of consciousness. All that pushing, kicking, negative thought and negative action make it impossible to achieve any degree of oneness, to perform any steps of the dance. It has been my experience that, for the rider at least, there are stages of consciousness that must be passed through in order to facilitate learning and healing; "one moves from the unconscious incompetent (where there is little, if any real connection, real understanding), to the conscious incompetent (where the student realizes there is or should be a healing interaction, but is insufficiently prepared to achieve it), on to the conscious competent (the student arrives at an ability to successfully interact physically, emotionally, and spiritually, but only through concentration and effort), and arrives at the unconscious competent (the student no longer has to do, he simply is)" At these levels, then, we need our horses to be our teachers, and, often we need others outside ourselves to help us realize our goals. A teacher, by his very being, is an example, a part of all of us. Sometimes, when in the presence of a teacher, you feel overwhelmed by a sense of simplicity and the power that comes with it. When I was in Portugal, many times I simply mimicked the Mestre. Just being him was enough. I discovered I could do things that I could never do before. I used to have very negative preconceived notions about Gurus. The meaning of the word Guru, however, is actually the one who dissipates darkness. And it is light, as well as lightness, which allows us to transcend our fears of happiness and the unknown. Trust allows healing energy to move into that space. Love and kindness coming from a clear picture of near perfection will guarantee we become comfortable there. Positive visualization no matter what happens is a sure way to stay there. It is often hard to realize, or accept, that you have been touched by divine energy. Don't let your goals become limitations.

Reflection

Speak to me of your time in the mountains –
 tell me your adventures, your stories
of companions and languorous days in the forest,
of the earth and her glories.

There is such beauty in your eyes,
 the sacred spark leaps
your essence, your life is reflected
 as the fire awakens.

This glowing fire abides now
 in my favorite space.
A space of warm, bright, encompassing love –
 the reflection in our eyes.

L'essence de la vie repose dans le mot "Voir." — Teilhard de Chardin

The whole of life lies in the verb "seeing". — Teilhard de Chardin

Someone said, "When cooking, you always forget one ingredient and the dish is ruined." Students often feel they are missing that one ingredient, especially the dressage students. Lack of knowledge pushes us to always want more, to never be satisfied with what we have. I ask you: More what? Which ingredient is missing? Imagine what your horse feels when you are never satisfied. Better to set simple goals in your training and achieve them. An instant quit after a successful achievement is the best reward you can offer your horse and yourself. More is the enemy of good. Keep your horse fresh and accepting. As his level of confidence and ability expands, so too will your own level of knowledge grow. For many, though, education multiplies fear; be careful, then, that your new-found knowledge leads not to new fears, but to new love, to new trust. The heart we are functioning with is a conditional heart: "I love 'if'...," "you love 'if'..." It is not our hearts, then, that we really mistrust, it is the conditionality. We crave unconditional love, Divine love. The child, the horse knows this love, the mind has not gotten in the way. Clear visualization of your goal, no matter how simple will help lead you to love and kindness, both of which

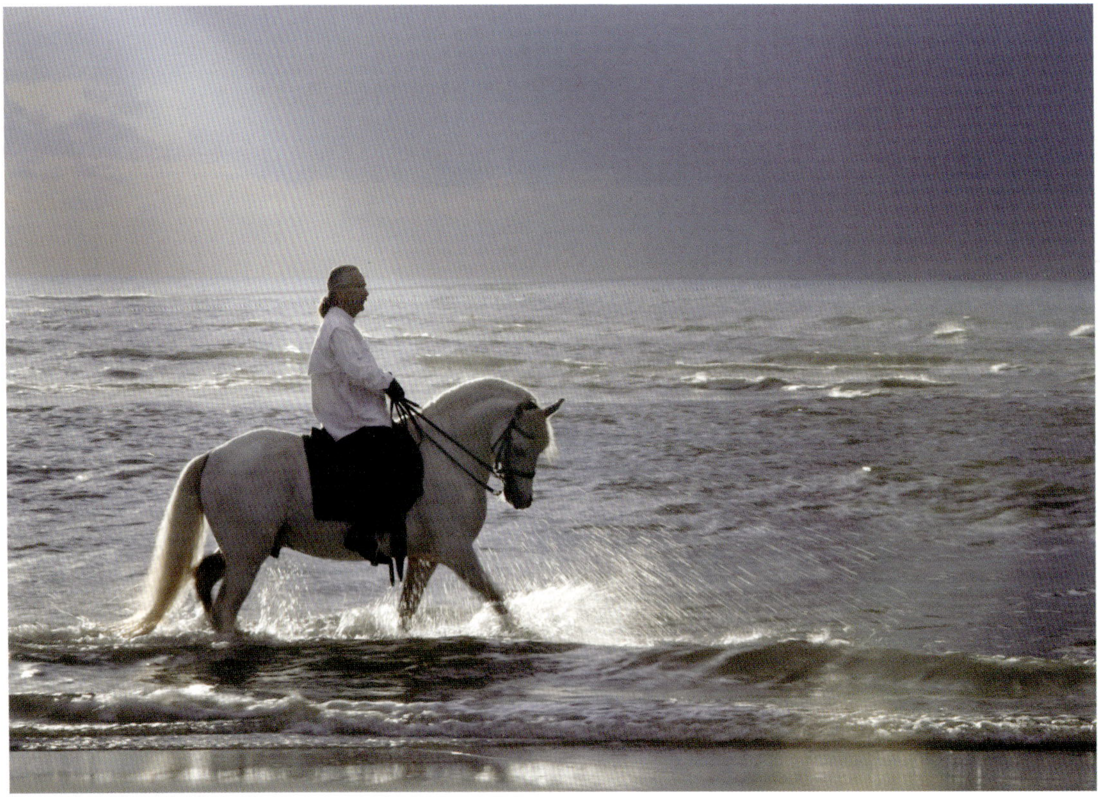

go a long way with horses ~ and people. When you find a sense of peace and comfort through knowledge, instead of fear or conditional love, you are ready to appreciate beauty, you are willing to share, you are following the recipe for success. Where then is the missing ingredient? What more can you ask for?

Our worst fear is not that we are inadequate, our deepest fear is that we are powerful beyond measure. It is our light, not our darkness that frightens us. We ask ourselves "who am I to be brilliant, gorgeous, talented, and fabulous?" Actually, who are you not to be? You are a child of God; your playing small does not serve the world. There is nothing enlightened about shrinking so that other people won't feel insecure around you.

Marianne Williamson

52

My Wish

I hear you in the stillness
of the forest as the snow softly falls,
  as the mist gently rises

I see you in the purity
of nature's pallette in every season,
 fresh greens and yellows, glowing reds
   and soothing blues

I feel you as the roots embrace the soil
and the soil nourishes life

I wish for you the blessings
of boundless joy in this
  and every season.

Dominique Barbier was born in France in 1950. In 1962, Dominique began his equine career at a Jesuit school in Poitiers, France. At 15, he attended Crabett Park School in England. There he received his British Horse Society Assistant Instructor (BHSAI). In 1972, Dominique returned to England to attend the Talland School of Equitation in Cirenchester, where Mrs. Molly Siveright, FBHS, DBHS, instructed him. He continued riding throughout Europe at numerous facilities in various disciplines, including jumping, three-day eventing, dressage, and steeple-chasing. Dominique then went to Portugal to study two years with Mestre Nuno Oliviera. Through his internship with Mestre Nuno Oliviera, Dominique learned to ride by perfecting his "mental and physical attitude". The experience became a turning point in his riding career and inspired his belief in keeping the horse light and happy; "la belle legerete a la Francaise". While in Portugal, Dominique purchased Dom Pasquale, Dom Giovanni, and Dom Jose. These Lusitano stallions were to be the first he would train to high school levels. In addition, Dom Giovanni learned to canter on the spot and to canter backwards.

Since immigrating to the United States, Dominique's teaching and passion for the "Art of Dressage" has reached many thousands of people in the United States, as well as North Africa, Europe, Asia, and Brazil. Ahead of his time, Dominique has been teaching the importance of mental communication and the understanding of the horse's nature for nearly forty years.

55

His critically acclaimed book, *Dressage for the New Age*, was revolutionary to the Dressage world when first published, with its look into the horse's psychology and well being as the cornerstones of training. *Dressage for the New Age*, now in its third edition in English, has also been published in French, Portuguese, and German. Dominique's award winning video series has helped thousands of riders who were unable to ride with him begin their journey to the "light side of riding". His next literary undertaking, Souvenir, was a journey through his previous years of teaching, illustrated by pictures of horses that he has trained, including notes from his teaching. "Sketches of the Equestrian Art" was created by Dominique and Jean Louis Sauvat, co-founder of the Versailles School of Equitation. *The Barbier Dressage Training Companion* was published in 2007 and quickly garnered awards and acclaim.

Dominique, along with his wife Debra, and daughters Domina and Tianna, reside in Northern California in the Sonoma Valley. He spends much of his time now, when not teaching throughout the world, in Brazil. His association with the Lusitano breeders in Brazil has allowed him to undertake another of his life's passions; spreading the love of the Lusitano horse to riders around the world. He shares his passion with students and riders through trips to Brazil and the importing of the finest Lusitanos bred today.

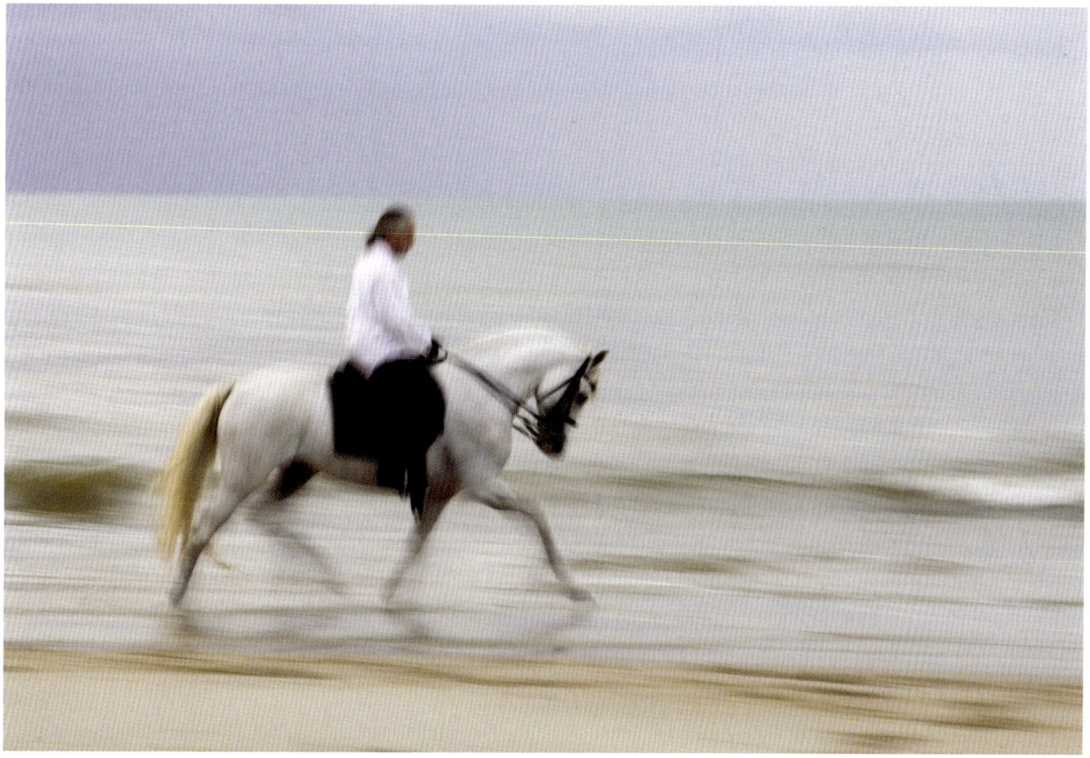

58

Keron Psillas was born in West Virginia in 1962, and has lived in Shepherdstown for most of her life. She was educated in local schools, but says that her most meaningful education has come through obserevation and inquiry. As a lover of horses, of books, of art, people, mystery and travel, Keron has crafted an emotionally and intellectually stimulating life by indulging these passions.

After 20 years as a parent and business owner, photography came into focus as an important creative outlet in 2004, while traveling in Scotland to research a book that she is developing. As the photos became more an expression of an impression or feeling, rather than a documentary recording, it was apparent that the images were as important to the project as the writing.

After a number of months living in Europe to focus solely on photography, Keron moved to Seattle and began two years tenure as the Director of the Art Wolfe Digital Photography Center. The access to industry professionals and renowned artists has facilitated her developing career as an image-editing and publishing consultant.

While continuing to learn from the Masters in the field, including Sam Abell, Jay Maisel, and Arthur Meyerson, and most importantly, her students, Keron is now instructing and leading trips worldwide, often with Dominique and Debra Barbier. She is represented by the Corbis and Danita Delimont agencies.

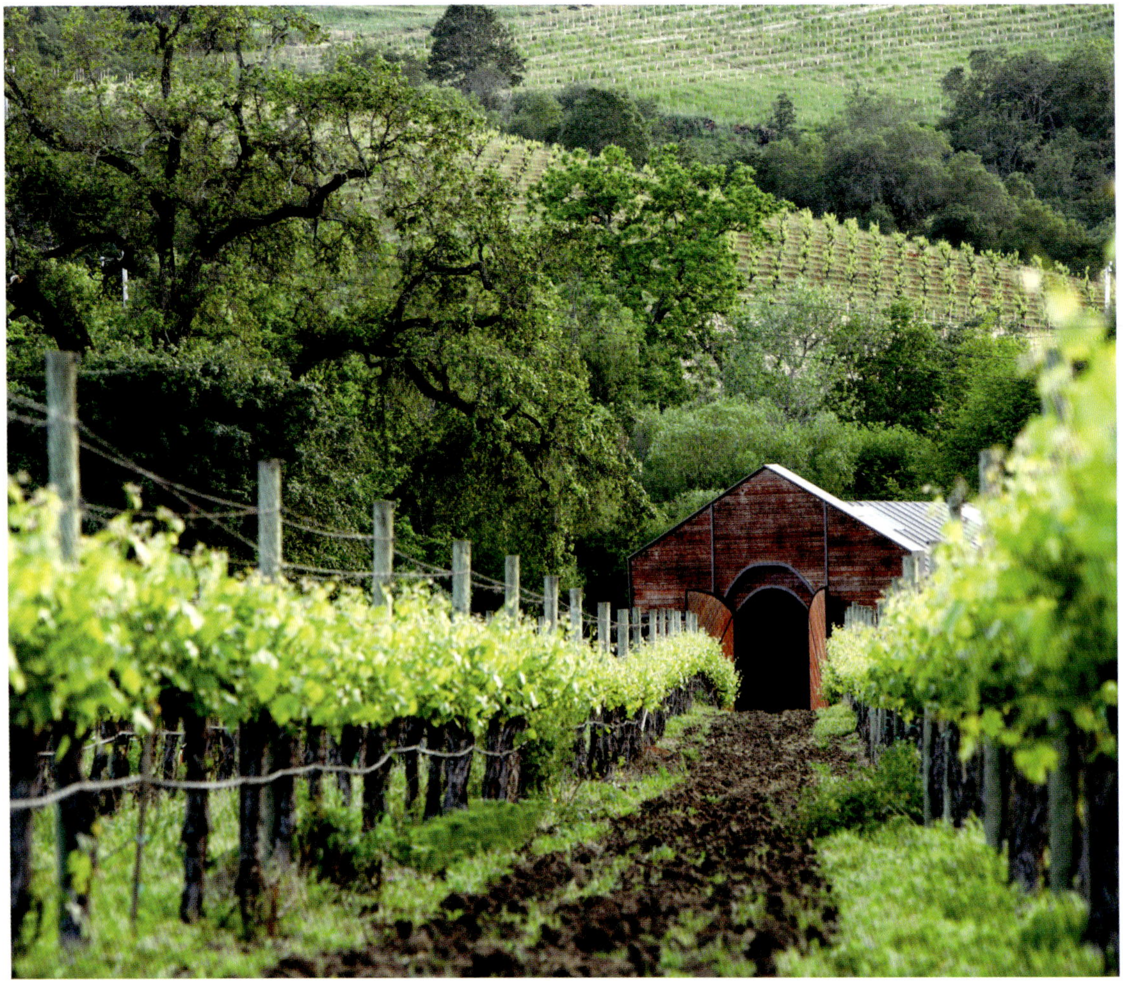

a true dance
   by Keelee for Debra and Dominique

It is not just a place to learn the art of dressage...
   it is a safe place, enveloped in love, to learn
to unlearn all that is not love, in riding in life...
   a preparation for what one may discover here.

It is not just a land of vineyards and wildlife...
   it is a reflection of who we are, a quiet mirror of
the true self
in all its perfection, a kind and soft reminder,
   a haven, a sheltered space where we may begin
to see the beauty and strength that lies within.

It is not just a place where we may go to escape...
   it is where quiet surroundings and stillness
place the fear we tried to escape
squarely in our faces, so that we will look,
and then we can finally see it is all just illusion.

It is not just a place of long and physically
exhausting days for a working student,
   it is a wearing away of an ego shell, through tears
sometimes, through resistance until it softens, until
we let go...and can finally see the true treasure, soft
and peaceful...always here, always now.

....a growing awareness of the strength and tenacity
within us to endure, despite physical and mental and
emotional weariness, an awareness of the stuff we are
made of, as we go toward what seems to be a goal
or a dream that we imagine horses can somehow fulfill...

Not completely aware of the magic at work,
   we are stripped away slowly,
at times feeling defeated. Yet as the tears come, there
stands the horse we are working, waiting, loving us.

62

The misty morning fog gently begins to lift,
   we are closer to something, it is clearing.
A heart opens, a soul clears, a healing...And in this clearing, a possibility appears of the true dance.

And yet, not completely aware of the orchestration of it all, we are magically brought closer to the heart of Horse. Not how we imagined it would happen, yet perfect still.

It is not just a building with horses and hay, stalls and mice...It is a barn filled with magic, hidden in every moment, if we but remember to stop...to listen...and see...the sounds of munching hay after having just fed breakfast soothe the heart, calm the mind, and remind us just to be. A soft muzzle, a look...

....And in those moments we can look into the big, warm eyes of one close by who sees clearly, always...and in those eyes, if there is less clutter in our own, we might feel a connection. We might just see ourselves. And maybe, just maybe, if we choose, we will do that thing all who are drawn to horses hope for...we will dance.

This is not just a place to learn to ride...it is a place infused with the joy of life, the wisdom of the heart. It is a magical and loving space, a scene respite from the world outside, allowing a clearing, to remember not only how to dance with a horse, but to dance with life's essence...with another of our Self...a true dance.

Acknowledgements

from Dominique:

to all the horses and the privilege to share my life with them

from Keron:

Ian, Jessica, and Will…I look forward to the unfolding of your lives. Thank you for your encouragement of mine.

Steve Forrest, my beloved wizard. Your guidance is fierce and true, always wrapped in love.

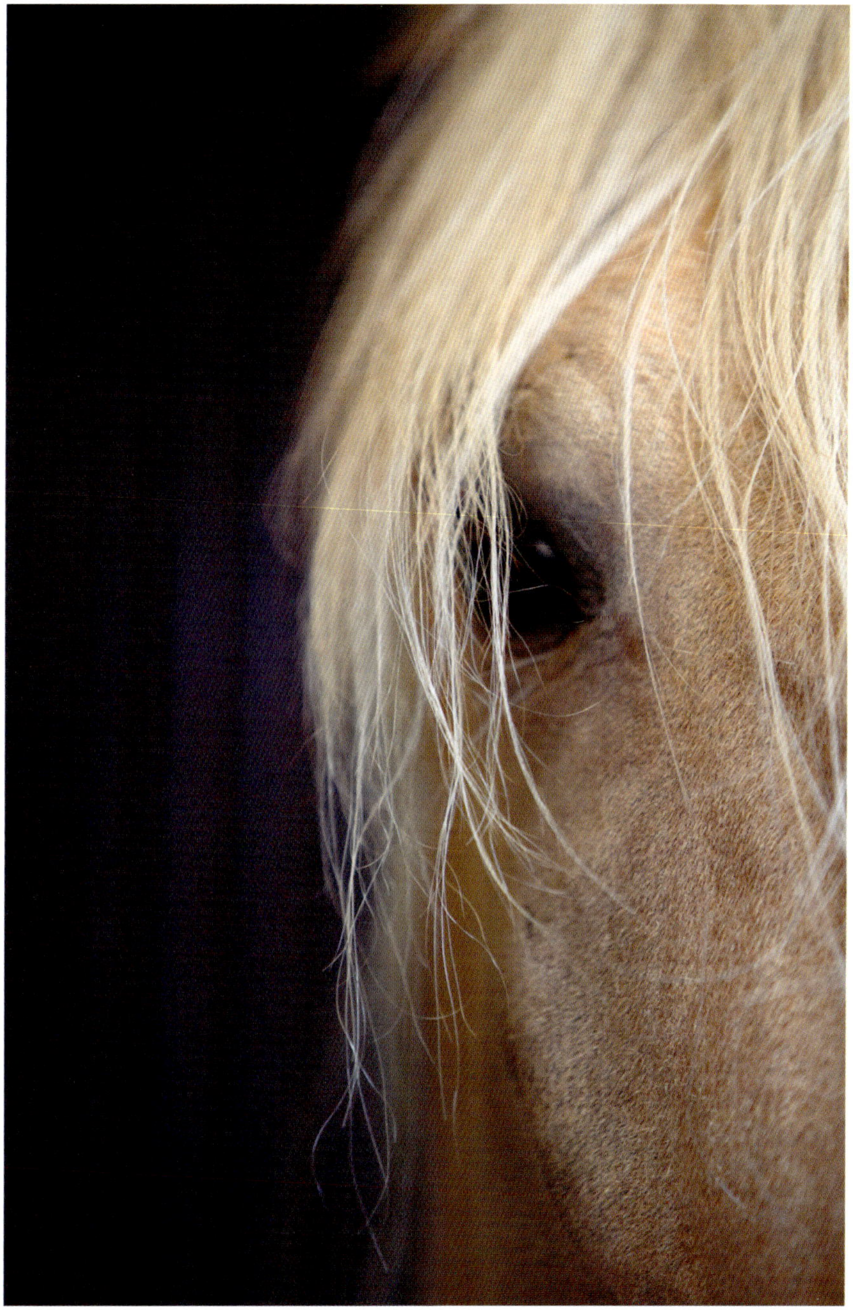

Photographs

cover, Dominique on Tobold, Chicago, 2010

half title, Bell, Barbier Farms, 2008

intro, Roberto on Vivaldi, Bahia, 2007

title, Dominique on Sedoso, Barbier Farms, 2005

7, Sparrow in Fountain in Palais Royale, Paris, 2006

8, Swallows, Southeast Passage, Alaska, 2006

10, Lillie, Barbier Farms, 2007

12, Spirit of Horse, Bahia, 2007

14, Dominique on Ultraje, Barbier Farms, 2007

16, Mirroring, Winchester, England, 2004

18, Dominique on Xodo, Barbier Farms, 2010

20, Ultraje, Barbier Farms, 2008

23, Melinda and Orador, Hope Township, New Jersey, 2006

24, Borgo Pinti, Florence, 2006

26, Eiffel Fleurs, Paris, 2006

28, Orador, Hope Township, New Jersey, 2006

30, Miguel on Suplicio, Bahia, 2007

32, Mare, Coudelaria Ilha Verde, Brazil, 2007

34, Dominique with Quilate, Barbier Farms, 2005

Photographs, continued

36, Poppy, Magnolia Gardens, South Carolina, 2008

38, Triunfo, Manege Santa Adelaide, Brazil, 2007

40, Detail from Neptune, Florence, 2006

42, Narsil, Barbier Farms, 2005

44, Lumiere, Delaware Water Gap, 2008

47, Dominique and Narsil, Barbier Farms, 2006

48, Dominique's Rose, Barbier Farms, 2006

50, Dawning, Bahia, 2007

52, Mist in Fall, Delaware Water Gap, 2008

55, Portrait, Barbier Farms, 2006

57, 1st Morning, Bahia, 2007

58, Winter Outing, by Denny Ccrosby, 2006

60, Vineyard, Barbier Farms, 2005

62, Narsil, Barbier Farms, 2009

65, Ultraje, Barbier Farms, 2009

68, Mousso, Barbier Farms, 2005

69, Detail, Angel, Opera Del Duomo, Florence, 2006

70, Miguel on Valiente, Bahia, 2007

71, Dominique on Sedoso, Barbier Farms, 2005

72, Dominique on Xamado do Top, Santa Adelaide, 2010

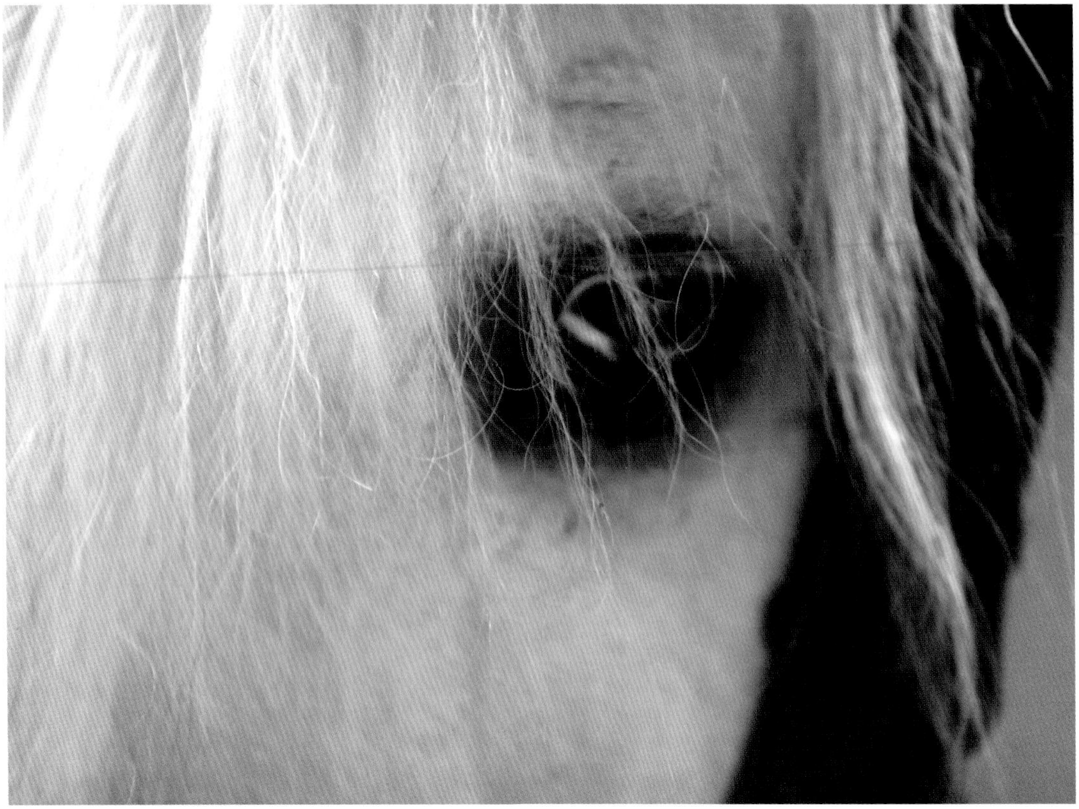

This edition of MEDITATION FOR TWO was set in Garamond Pro. The display type is Cezanne, with a nod to Dominique's French heritage and to link and respect the arts of handwriting, photography, and bookmaking, as well as the influence of the painting Masters on the history of photography.

70

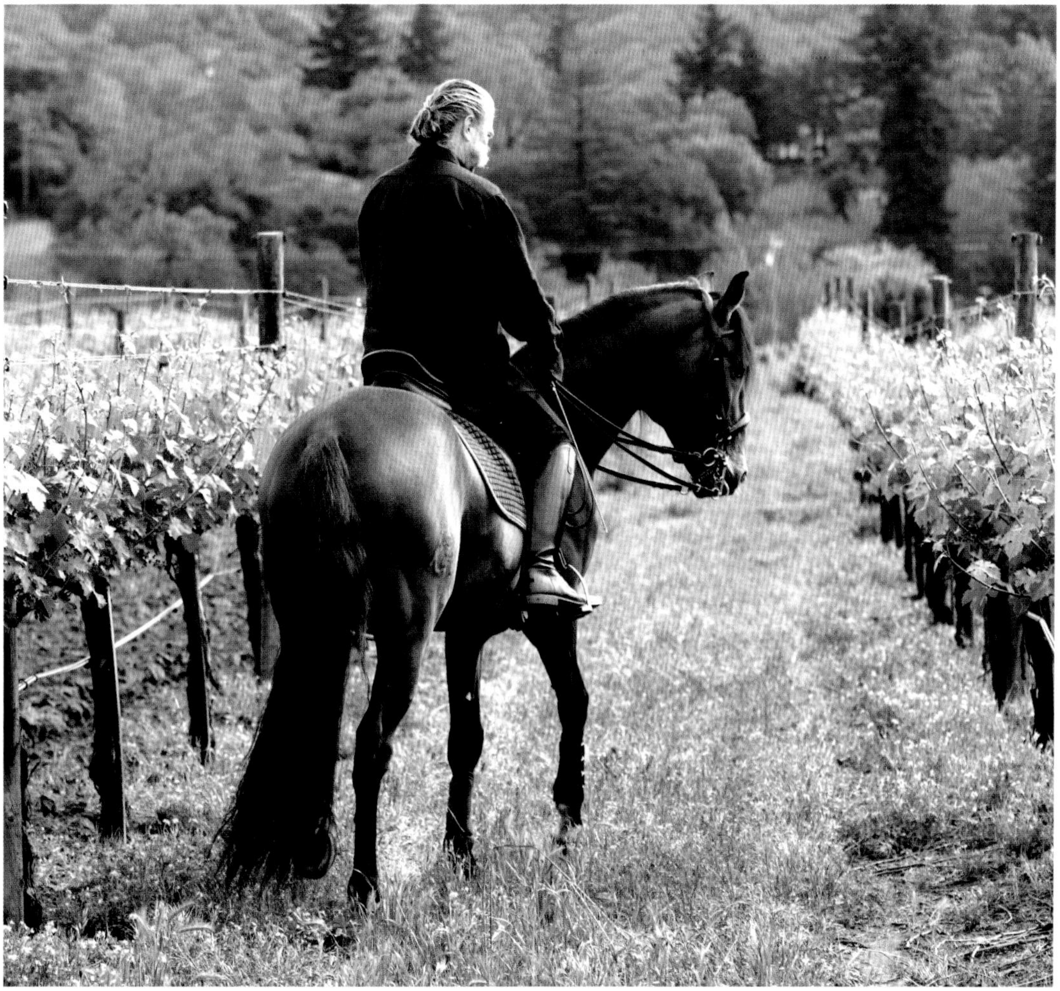

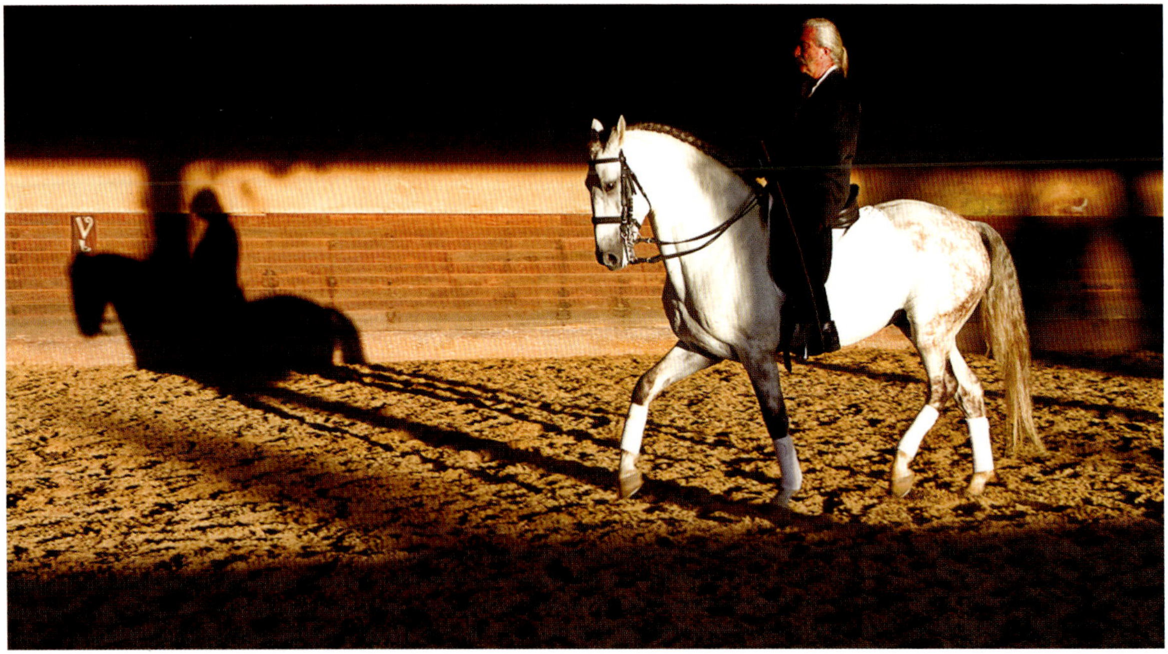